WordTOOLS For Business

Vol. 2

Harnessing the
Power of Words!

Carol L Rickard, LCSW

Well YOUniversity® Publications

Sign up now!

To be sure to get our weekly motivational & inspirational quotes and stories!

ThePowerOfWordsEQuote.com

Copyright © 2017 Carol L. Rickard

All Licensing by Well YOUniversity, LLC

All rights reserved.

ISBN-13: 978-1-947745-03-2

WordTools for Business Vol. 2

Harnessing the Power of Words!

by Carol L Rickard, LCSW

© Copyright 2015 Well YOUniversity Publications

ISBN 13: 978-1-947745-03-2

All rights reserved.

No part of this book may be reproduced for resale, redistribution, or any other purposes (including but not limited to eBooks, pamphlets, articles, video or audiotapes, & handouts or slides for lectures or workshops).

Licenses to reproduce these materials for those and any other purposes must be obtained from the author and Well YOUniversity.

888 LIFE TOOLS (543-3866)

Carol@WellYOUniversity.com

Welcome!

My 1st WordTool came to me in 2006 when doing a group with my patients. How could I get them to *welcome* change in their lives?

Creating **H**ealthy **A**nd **N**ew **G**rowth **E**xperiences!

From there it's been an onward journey! Most of them are inspired by persons or situations. My hope is to create Ah-Ah moments that can help change a life!

They are officially called "Artinyms", which is Sanskrit for "describe".

On the back of each wordtool is a question for you to answer should you choose to!

~To Living Well TODAY! ~

Carol

ADAPT	1	FAILURE	31
ASK	3	FOCUS	33
ATTITUDE	5	GRATEFUL	35
AWARE	7	GROW	37
CAN'T	9	IMAGINE	39
CHANGE	11	INSPIRED	41
CLARITY	13	LEARN	43
COMPROMISE	15	MARKET	45
CONSISTENT	17	NEEDS	47
DEBT	19	PLANS	49
DO	21	PROMOTE	51
DOUBT	23	REACT	53
EFFORT	25	RISK	55
EVALUATE	27	START	57
FACT	29	TRUST	59

Sign up now!

To be sure to get our weekly motivational & inspirational quotes and stories!

ThePowerOfWordsEQuote.com

A

Deliberate

Adjustment

Providing

Transformation

COPYRIGHT 2017 & Licensed by Well YOUniversity, LLC

When is a time when you *adapted* and how did it go?

Acquire

Self

Knowledge

COPYRIGHT 2017 & Licensed by Well YOUniversity, LLC

What have you always wanted to know but were afraid to *ask*?

Adjusting

Thinking

To

Intentionally

Take

Us

Direction

Excellence

COPYRIGHT 2017 & Licensed by Well YOUniversity, LLC

How would you describe your *attitude*?

Does it need adjusting?

Actively

Work

At

Recognizing

Existence

COPYRIGHT 2017 & Licensed by Well YOUniversity, LLC

How would your life be different if you were more ***aware*** every day!

Counts

As

Not

'

Trying

COPYRIGHT 2017 & Licensed by Well YOUniversity, LLC

What is it you have been telling yourself that you **CAN'T** do? Have you even tried?

Creating

Healthy

And

New

Growth

Experiences

COPYRIGHT 2017 & Licensed by Well YOUniversity, LLC

What are some important *changes* you could make in your life that would pay off BIG?

Clearly

Looking

At

Resources

Important

To

You

COPYRIGHT 2017 & Licensed by Well YOUniversity, LLC

What are some of the areas in your life where you need more *clarity*?

Create

Opportunities

Merging

Peoples

Requirements

Only

Making

It

Serve

Everyone

COPYRIGHT 2017 & Licensed by Well YOUniversity, LLC

When was a time you made a ***compromise***?

What was the outcome?

Concentrate

On

Not

Stopping

Instead

Strengthening

The

Effort

Needed

Today

COPYRIGHT 2017 & Licensed by Well YOUniversity, LLC

What do you need to be *consistent* with that has been difficult for you to do in the past?

Doing

Excessively &

Becoming

Trapped

COPYRIGHT 2017 & Licensed by Well YOUniversity, LLC

Do you have any **debt** in your life?

How is it impacting your life?

Direct

Opportunity

© 2017 & Licensed by Well YOUniversity, LLC

What is it that you still want to *DO* in your lifetime?

Dwelling

On

Unfounded

Beliefs &

Thoughts

COPYRIGHT 2017 & Licensed by Well YOUniversity, LLC

What has *doubt* stopped you from doing?

What would you do if it didn't exist?

Engage

Full

Force

On

Reaching

Targets

COPYRIGHT 2017 & Licensed by Well YOUniversity, LLC

What are some goals you have that could use some *effort* towards?

Extremely

Valuable

Activity

Letting

Us

Assess

True

Effectiveness

COPYRIGHT 2017 & Licensed by Well YOUniversity, LLC

Do you tend to be someone who *evaluates* decisions? What have you learned?

Face
A
Concrete
Truth

COPYRIGHT 2017 & Licensed by Well YOUniversity, LLC

Are there any *facts* you are facing a hard time trying to deal with?

Find

An

Important

Lesson

Using

Real

Experiences

COPYRIGHT 2017 & Licensed by Well YOUniversity, LLC

What are some important lessons you have learned from *failure*?

Fix

Our

Concentration

Until

Successful

COPYRIGHT 2017 & Licensed by Well YOUniversity, LLC

What are you planning to use your *focus* to achieve?

Giving

Respect

And

Thanks

Everyday

For

Unbelievable

Life!

COPYRIGHT 2017 & Licensed by Well YOUniversity, LLC

Make a list of all the things you are *grateful* for having in your life:

Gradually

Recognize

Our

Way

COPYRIGHT 2017 & Licensed by Well YOUniversity, LLC

What are some of the ways in which you have **grown** over the last year? Last 5 years?

Incredible

Mental

Activity

Generating

Ideas

Not

Existing!

COPYRIGHT 2017 & Licensed by Well YOUniversity, LLC

If you were to let It run wild, what would you *imagine* your life to look like 1 year from now?

I

Now

See

Possibility

In

Reaching &

Engaging

Daily

COPYRIGHT 2017 & Licensed by Well YOUniversity, LLC

Who have been some of the people in your life that have *inspired* you?

Link
Education
And
Resources
Needed!

COPYRIGHT 2017 & Licensed by Well YOUniversity, LLC

What is it that you don't know how to do that you'd like to *learn*?

Messages

Aimed &

Reaching

Key

Established

Targets

COPYRIGHT 2017 & Licensed by Well YOUniversity, LLC

What steps are you taking to *market*? Who is your established target customer?

Necessary

Elements

Enabling

Daily

Survival

COPYRIGHT 2017 & Licensed by Well YOUniversity, LLC

What are your life *needs*?

What are your business's needs?

Purposely

Laid

Activity

Necessary

Succeed

COPYRIGHT 2017 & Licensed by Well YOUniversity, LLC

Do you have any **plans** for the coming year? If so, what are they? If not, why not?

Purposely

Reach

Others

Making

Opportunities

To

Empower

COPYRIGHT 2017 & Licensed by Well YOUniversity, LLC

What is the opportunity you have to share with others? What's stopping you from *promoting*?

Release

Emotions

And

Create

Trouble

COPYRIGHT 2017 & Licensed by Well YOUniversity, LLC

When was a time in your life where you *reacted* & made the situation worse?

Result

Is

Seldom

Known

COPYRIGHT 2017 & Licensed by Well YOUniversity, LLC

What are you willing to *risk* in the pursuit of success?

Swiftly

Take

Action

Reaching

Targets

COPYRIGHT 2017 & Licensed by Well YOUniversity, LLC

What have been some of the actions or goals you have not **started** yet?

To

Risk

Uncertainty

Seeking

Togetherness

COPYRIGHT 2017 & Licensed by Well YOUniversity, LLC

What does a person need to show you in order for you to *trust* them?

About the Author

Carol L Rickard, LCSW, TTS, of Hopewell, NJ is founder & CEO of WellYOUniversity, LLC, a global health education company dedicated *to empowering individuals with the tools and supports to achieve lifelong wellness & recovery.*

Also known as **America's Wellness Ambassador**, Carol is a dynamic & engaging speaker who brings to life practical / useful solutions. She is a weekly contributor for Esperanza Magazine; written 13 books on stress and wellness, had a guest appearance on Dr. Oz last year

She is also the creator & host of a 30-minute wellness show on Princeton TV - **The WELL YOU Show** which current episodes are aired on Mondays at 6:00pm EST & Sundays at 8:30am EST and can be watched at PrincetonTV.org.

All episodes available at: **www.TheWELLYOUShow.com**

Get more of Carol at:

Twitter: ***@wellYOUlife***

"Like us" @ www.FaceBook.com/WellYOUniversity

Have Carol Speak at Your Next Event!

Get more information about how you can have Carol speak at your organization, event, or conference.

Go to: www.CarolLRickard.com

Or call: 888 Life Tools (543-3866)

Carol's Other Books

Getting Your Mind to Mind You
ANGER – A Simple & Practical Approach
Help – How to Help Those Who DON'T Want it
Selfness – Simple Self-Care Secrets
Stress Eating – How to STOP Using Food to Cope
Stretched Not Broken – Caregiver's Stress
The Caregiver's Toolbox
Transforming Illness to Wellness
Putting Your Weight Loss on Auto
The Benefits of Smoking
Moving Beyond Depression
LifeTools – How to Manage Life
Creating Compliance
Relapse Prevention

Please visit us at:

www.WellYOUniversity.com

Sign up for weekly motivational e-quote!

Check out our upcoming FREE webinars!

Learn more about our training programs.

Email us your success story at:

Success@WellYOUniversity.com

We'd like to ask for your feedback

Please check out the next page
if this book has been HELPFUL for you!

We'd love to hear from you!

Feedback Card

Please take a moment & provide us some feedback about the book you just read & how you feel *it benefited YOU!*

_____

_____

_____

_____

Tear along here

Name: _____

Best Phone #: _____

Can we use your comments in our publicity materials?

Yes / No

If OK with you, what's the best time to call you:_____

Thank You!

Scan or take a picture & email:

Carol@WellYOUniversity.com

Snail mail: Carol Rickard

5 Zion Rd., Hopewell, NJ 08535

www.ingramcontent.com/pod-product-compliance
Lightning Source LLC
LaVergne TN
LVHW051209080426
835512LV00019B/3175